MORE TROUBLE W

.

More Trouble with the Obvious is the 1980 Lamont Poetry
Selection of the Academy of American Poets

From 1954 through 1974 the Lamont Poetry Selection
supported the publication and distribution of twenty
first books of poems. Since 1975 this distinguished award
has been given for an American poet's second book.
Judges for 1980: William Harmon, Maxine Kumin,
Richard Shelton.

POEMS BY

Michael Van Walleghen

MORE TROUBLE
WITH THE OBVIOUS

UNIVERSITY OF ILLINOIS PRESS

Urbana Chicago London

Publication of this work was supported in part by a
grant from the Illinois Arts Council, a state agency

Manufactured in the United States of America

These poems first appeared in the following
magazines:
A Lake Superior Journal: "The Last Hangover in
  March," "The Escape Artist"
Ploughshares: "Painting the Picture," "Crab-
  apples," "Some Observations by a Newlywed"
The Southern Review: "The Sibyl at Snug Harbor,"
  "Fun at Crystal Lake"
Ascent: "Reading the *I Ching*," "How the Fireman's
  Widow Became a Wasp," "The Fisherman,"
  "Mistakes"
The Hudson Review: "Walking the Baby to the
  Liquor Store," "Driving into Enid," "Do Not
  Dump Dead Animals," "More Trouble with the
  Obvious," "Arizona Movies"
Prairie Voices: Poets of Illinois (Illinois Arts
  Council): "The Honeymoon of the Muse"

"Arizona Movies" subsequently appeared in *The
Pushcart Prize No. II: Best of the Small Presses*
(1977-78 edition)

Library of Congress Cataloging in Publication Data

Van Walleghen, Michael, 1938-
  More trouble with the obvious.

  I. Title.
PS3572.A545M6   811'.54   80-24215
ISBN 0-252-00864-2 (cloth)
ISBN 0-252-00865-0 (paper)

for Pamela
and Emily Lynn

CONTENTS

I

THE SIBYL AT SNUG HARBOR

The fish are biting
or they're not. Birds
wade the shallows here
in sunlight, or otherwise
appear for ghostly moments
in the fog, and the tides
move either in or out
the way they should
regardless of the weather,
for this is just Snug Harbor
where we fish. Today,
the perfectly ordinary sky
is blue, the windless bay
is blue, and the snowy egret
stalking minnows near the shore
seems somehow almost fake
and planted there,
like a lawn decoration,
the property of a Mrs. Garrison
walking over in hip-boots,
her voice midwestern, flat-out,
and friendly as the weather.

Yesterday, however, her husband
caught a strange fish here,
a fat eel or dogfish sort of thing
no one could identify. Disgusted,
they threw it back; whereupon
she was utterly amazed
to see it clumsily attacked
by an enormous sea gull
who tried a full hour

to swallow it. Furthermore,
last night, she dreamt of it,
and her retired husband,
who has diabetes, arthritis,
and serious heart trouble,
was kept awake till dawn
by the sexual racket
of wandering, ferocious cats—
all of which goes nowhere, is apropos
of something she forgets . . .
"and in the morning"
her husband says, grabbing
at my arm, "the goddamn things
jump right out at you
from the garbage bin."

FUN AT CRYSTAL LAKE

After a day of whitecaps
and the threat of tornadoes
the lake turns calm again
a few mayflies begin to hatch
and by late afternoon even
the moon is visible.
              Perhaps
things will work out after all.
Perhaps there will be fireworks
later on, or maybe a barbecue,
and if everyone behaves, maybe
a quick ride just before dark
in the speedboat!
                  I hope so.
I like happy endings sometimes
don't you? Take the kid
I caught just yesterday
for instance, at the beach
across the lake, stalking
a chipmunk with a brick.
                    He was
"just having fun" he said
and that was that. No doubt
the people at the fancy lodge
are likewise having fun, especially
the man with the fireworks,
the motorcycle kids,

and whoever it is
who laughs so hysterically
after each explosion. In any case
what good does it do to worry?
What good did it ever do? Take
this dragonfly for instance
eating a bee
                on a red washcloth
or the man with the speedboat
yelling at his brainless son
again, for walking pigeon-toed
for having a sad face
an ugly lip, a forehead
like his mother's.

A man has a problem so overwhelming he throws the *I Ching* right out the window. What good is it? When he walks into a room he does not see his wife. When he steps outside he sees a woodpecker pecking a cement lightpole. Misfortune. Why bother to continue? Yesterday, a mouse kept jumping up and falling down again *plop!* in the paper bag beneath the sink, and the day before that, he thought he saw a hand or suffocating bird flutter whitely up in an attic window. In continuing thus, one sees humiliation. One sees perhaps a greasy cocker spaniel sleeping on the sidewalk or a fat kid throwing a tennis ball soaked in mud against his family's brand-new aluminum siding. Why is the truth always so difficult and miserable? One sees the fat kid smiling at his little brother . . . then sister slams into the house and breaks the front door window. No blame. No blame. The heavy woman on the porch puffs deeply on her cigarette and rolls her blue blue eyes. The man taking a walk looks up too — surprised at how things go, smiling for the first time in days, reassured.

TELEMACHIAD

My father
the long-distance swimmer
is asleep, leaving me
in charge of everything:
the house with its one
dead tree, stray hubcaps
filling up with water,
his oildrums and fenders,
the two dead pigs
hanging side by each
in our dark garage,
and all summer afternoon
nothing happens. He continues
sleeping on the couch,
grinds his teeth, sweats,
and just keeps bravely on
I suppose, dreaming sharks,
jellyfish, exhaustion,
and the plain misery
of cold water. My job
is easier, is simply being
nine years old, bored stiff,
the pissed-off little prince
who thinks he runs this place,
with its falling-down garage,
its one dead tree, the pigs
I always got to watch
getting frantically butchered
in the basement, and mother
busy in the kitchen, singing

like a goddess, pigeons
cooing in the rain-loud
dark pavilions
of some Belle Isle.

THE GREAT CORNFLAKE
MYSTERY

I've been on this case
for years, my dark family's
private eye, surmising
lamp, hotplate, mirror,
the dirty curtains blowing out
and in again, haircurlers,
underwear, the bus tickets
around there somewhere—
bureau, suitcase, bed,
the hectic, girlish clutter
of a room I keep thinking
I remember—a completely
ordinary room, cheap
but facing the sunny
side of some busy street
above a Chinese laundry
and not too far from work,
the grocery store, the cheaper
uptown movies—a room
you were lucky to afford
in 1933, and what's more
this was Hollywood, heaven
for awhile; a good waitress
could almost live on tips
out there, and one meal
a day, at least, was free.
But I don't know . . . all
I've got to work on

is a photograph of mother
and her girl friend Marion
eating cornflakes. It all
adds up to cornflakes . . .
and two girls so pretty
they might have made the movies
but instead were out of work
flat busted and really hungry
having their picture taken.

II

HOW THE FIREMAN'S WIDOW
BECAME A WASP

The agent of her metamorphosis is still a mystery although intelligent guessing points inevitably at fire. Then too, her lifelong reputation for "waspishness" is a matter of record—the theme of much firehouse gossip and speculation. What drove her husband, for instance, to risk his life so precipitously at fire after fire? The answer seems obvious to anyone who knew her even slightly. But for the sake of clear argument, and to strike quickly at the heart of the matter, it might help to reconstruct the immediate, transmogrifying event.

Some boys have found a wasps' nest in a field. Of one mind, as if by instinct, they start throwing stones at it . . . then it becomes necessary to poke at it with sticks. Finally, after one of them is stung, the littlest boy runs home and gets the gasoline. The situation is simple, classic. *The field is on fire! The field is on fire! Boys have set the field on fire!* You can easily see, I think, the timelessness of this— how it might be happening anywhere. But the fireman's widow is frantic. Her house is nearly adjacent to the field and if the wind should change, if the fire should get as far as the peach tree. . . .

The widow puts on her husband's hat and rubber boots. She alerts the neighbors, gets out the garden hose, and by the time the firemen arrive, she appears to have everything under control. She even persuades the fire chief to apologize for not arriving sooner, then stings him expertly with memories of her own alacritous and legendary husband who died fighting a routine fire much like this one. After that, one by one, the firemen are obliged to shake

15

her hand and leave her standing there like some freakishly dwindled nuclear survivor in the smoking field, a figure so diminutive and poignant, so entirely pathetic, the peach tree seems to droop a little out of sympathy.

As someone who has spent considerable time investigating the matter, it's my opinion that from this moment the transformation from widow to wasp was irreversible. As a matter of fact, no one I've talked to remembers ever seeing her again in human form. For the children, who were subsequently caught and punished, the event has naturally assumed, over the years, the character of cautionary parable or fable, although none of them are quite sure of the exact lesson to be learned there. Most of them have continued to play with fire and refuse to understand the occasional ferocity of certain women.

THE HONEYMOON
OF THE MUSE

*You're right. There's nothing
much to see out here but corn*

*and soybeans. Wake me up
when we get to Denver.* Yawning

this, the tired muse gives up
but Illinois goes on forever

with detours through Homer,
Sadorus, Villa Grove . . .

towns nestled at the foot
of nothing —and therefore

precarious somehow, fitfully
alpine, as if the sky itself

might suddenly collapse
and wipe them out entirely.

*Are we there yet? Where's
the meadow, the hillside,*

*the shepherd with his flute?
Let's stop and ask directions.*

Poor kid. She thinks Denver
is a kind of honeymoon resort

located high on the slopes
of Mount Parnassus. She thinks

I'm rich and the airplane roar
of my broken muffler means simply

that my car can also fly. Why
not? She can believe anything.

So here we are slowing down
for Villa Grove . . . two scarce blocks

of houses, body shops and shattered
Chinese elms. No Denver certainly

but rare enough, a jewel really,
set high in the rugged mountains

of central Illinois. "Look . . ."
I whisper, kissing her perfect ear,

"there's a liquor store that's open
and a vacancy at the Villa Pines!"

THE ESCAPE ARTIST

The trick is somehow
not to be afraid . . .
but this time, again,
when the lifelines snap,
he can't remember it,
and just drifts off, sideways,
under months of ice
in his chained-up trunk,
a cold blue fetus
tied and handcuffed
like a gangster's corpse,
a fistula of dead nerve
so altogether witless
that before he's even picked
the first, tiniest lock, fumbling
hairpins underwater, the cops
will have cleared the bridge
and let the grave-sized hole
through which he dropped
freeze over. Of course
it's hopeless! A fact
lugubrious as pigeons
cooing in the rain
when he gets home, a screwball
straight from Gogol's Overcoat
waving his last obituary
like another poem
at the white houses
and whispering "it's me, it's me"
to no one who remembers.

MISTAKES

You've lost your key
and the landlord is sound asleep.

No . . . it's worse than that,
it's the wrong house entirely.

It's even the wrong street.
It's seventy below zero

on this street, your car
is buried in the snow,

and the river of smoke
billowing south-southeast

from the stove factory
means absolutely nothing.

You're not going to make it
that's all. Pretty soon

you will want to lie down
with mother in the snow

and dream of being born.
But not right now. Right now

the stars are telling you
their secrets. They speak

a kind of frantic Morse code . . .
they sound like a heart attack

or some freezing bird
fumbling at the porchlight.

I suppose he thinks
to land out there

in the galactic wind
on the bare bulb

and eventually get warm.
That's a mistake.

THE LAST HANGOVER
IN MARCH

By mid-morning,
eyelids still fluttering
like frantic birds,
I've escaped the house
of the hanged man,
the night of Sundays
in Detroit, the Detroit
newsboy without arms
and his frozen papers
to deliver, and settled
for the fool, the drunken
weak-eyed ne'er-do-well
who's squandered everything,
who's lost baronial estates
and the copra plantations,
hat factories, silver mines —
O, everything in fact . . .
except this life, this crust
of stale bread, this morning
with its budding maples
and the strange coincidence
of equinox and crocus
blooming near the fence
in the reckless light
of another century.

III

CONCERNING THE RECENT MARRIAGE
OF AN UNIMPORTANT MAN TO
AN UNIMPORTANT GIRL

> "Since your friends are like that, Georg,
> you shouldn't ever have got engaged at all."
> —Kafka's "The Judgement"

It's nice being married
but what about my old friend
who's presently going to pieces
somewhere in Russia? So what
if the lavender crocus are up
or the peonies have started?
His loose front door bangs
just as stupidly as ever
and the trees are furious
at their own reflections
which repeat incessantly
everything they say,
like lunatics, raving now
in all the shuddering windows
of the shit-brown house
across the street. It happens
too, that the police are coming
to ask him a few questions . . .
and stupidly, because death
is just another word
he can't believe he's saying,
he'll keep on saying it

25

until they notice Brutus,
his crippled German shepherd,
eating someone's tiny corpse
wrapped in paper near the curb.

A man like that, a bachelor
like that . . . so what
if presently I have a wife
in high heels and torn panty hose
making up the bed? Marriage
is against the law in Russia
and there are corpses everywhere,
some of them quite young. So what
if the lavender crocus are up
or that my wife insists on singing
half undressed, some pointless
little Russian song of spring?
My old friend is going crazy
and his worried, hang-dog look
haunts all the darkened windows
of my new estate —ramshackle
it's true, after all these years,
but still the same old place,
hidden as it always was
beside the reedy millpond —
where sometimes someone lovely
brought her cows to drink . . .
her dog was black and white.
Some of the cows
had bells.

THE FISHERMAN

For nearly a month he had been having dreams in which
he appeared to himself as someone he didn't like, some-
one he couldn't trust —and waking up he felt hysterical,
dull, dishonest and ashamed. But his wife thought that
perhaps he had been working too hard and that maybe
he ought to go fishing. He didn't particularly want to go
fishing —he knew things were more serious than that —but
the next morning before five o'clock he was dressed and
driving to the river.

He had been awake all night, and now, in his exhaustion,
the river appeared a little too familiar, the hard clay path
down to the water too predictably slick and dangerous.
He was sure he had dreamt about this place. Perhaps he
would sink into quicksand or miss his step and be swept
away by the current. He can't remember now how it
finally goes . . . but the path, certainly, seems something
he remembers —also, the glittering cave of trees and the
greasy, treacherous look of water bulging over stones.

Now he remembers he must throw a little wooden minnow
along the edge of some fallen trees. The minnow is painted
silver with terrified yellow eyes and he must throw it out
over and over again, watching it return from deep water
like something really alive, wounded, frantic and pursued.
He has dreamt this dream so often —himself pursued,
himself the fisherman —he can hardly breathe. And then,
when the fish hits, it's like waking up to a phone call he
thought he'd answered already in his sleep.

The startled, headlong heaviness of the thing! But there's
no question of ever landing it . . . only the heavy instant

27

pulling him toward the dark before the line breaks—and afterwards, the whole forest humming implacably as a dial tone after someone loved has just hung up. He sits down and can't believe it. He sits down like a man overwhelmed with mortgages, cracked foundations and fallen gutters. And he can't believe the bluejay either, hopping toward him down the muddy bank like a mechanical toy—or that his wife is really seeing someone else.

SOME OBSERVATIONS
BY A NEWLYWED

Someone you don't know
parks his blue pickup
in front of your house
and sits there smoking:

then he drinks something,
and sure enough, pretty soon,
a small, anxious-looking woman
with black hair shows up,

her rings and fancy coat
at odds with everything —
but who cares? They kiss,
look around, kiss again,

then, suddenly desperate,
she brushes back her hair
and ducks entirely down
beside him on the seat.

You know what's going on:
you're watering the plants
while he pretends to read
the paper. Your wife

is busy down the basement.
Someone you don't know
is looking at his watch.
Someone else is cooking supper.

Meanwhile, it's snowing here,
almost dark; and love, love
is still impossible, outrageous,
everything you thought it was:

your wife coming up
to check the mail,
make coffee, throw
the birds some toast.

TERMITES

I'm down the basement with the termite man. He's showing me three thousand dollars worth of damage: beams and crossbeams that need to be replaced, stanchions so comically rotten he can't imagine how our floors stay up. Brushing with his flashlight at some stubborn webs above the furnace he tells me of houses collapsing in the middle of the night, housewives falling through their own kitchens. He hands me little bits of wood that crumble into powder and says I'm lucky, *lucky*, he caught all this when he did. In his white coat, staring at his clipboard, he could be my doctor, anyone's doctor. "Yes," he might be saying, "yes, the slides *are* positive but the blood count still looks good." He wants to operate immediately. He thinks the generally slow development of a whole broad profile of symptoms puts the odds on our side. But at this stage, of course, time is crucial —a matter perhaps of even a few days.

It's best, I suppose, to take such news philosophically — which is to say one should avoid thinking about it. Termites, after all, are a joke, and a man who thinks too much about them risks being trivial and vulgar, a cartoon. This is a serious world and I'm damn lucky to have a house, I know that much. And more to the point, everyone I know is healthy. But I wander around anyway, from room to room, feeling the house shake and trying to distinguish the fine tremors of the furnace from the steadier fibrillation of the hot-water heater, the refrigerator . . . until, by suppertime, made dizzy by cigars, anxiety and too much whiskey, I stand precariously up in a room full of chairs —afraid, if I sat down, of being someone else, someone who watched TV seriously and weighed four hundred pounds. As it is, I prefer being a guest here, a man leaning on a bookcase, smoking a cigar, refusing to relax or even speak.

By bedtime, of course, I'm afraid of everything. Like Bartleby, I'd prefer to have nothing to do with termites. I'd prefer to lie down with my face to the wall and think of nothing at all. But the wall is full of termites. Termites, vulgar as they are, have multiplied astronomically in the crawl space underneath the porch, then migrated to the basement. And now I can hear them in the woodwork. I can hear my father saying how only a man who was deaf and blind could buy a house so shaky and infested, so obviously doomed. I can hear my father-in-law, a chief in the fire department, telling this story to his friends — his hands white with anger around a coffee cup, a poisonous froth of *Red Man* tobacco spit jumping from his lip when he gets to the part about his daughter falling through the kitchen. So much for sympathy. So much for understanding and forgiveness.

As if these termites were all my fault! As if, in the healthy prime of life, I had nothing better to do than to keep on checking down the basement every five minutes for termites! But what could I expect? It seems a man beset by termites is not a real man at all. No doubt his wife would be better off without him . . . maybe his daughter would feel better too. Who needs a father who gets dizzy all the time and weighs four hundred pounds? Therefore, one stares for hours at a cheap clock radio glowing in the dark — stares until it's almost daylight in the swamp, or, in the high bright rooms of the dying, a wind that's

almost warm puffs up the white curtains. Perhaps *that*
lifts the heart. Then a phantom jogger slaps by on his way
around the world — God's messenger, fleet-footed Mer-
cury, repeating the news that any second now the
exterminators could come knocking . . . followed by the
weather, the sound of light rain, the leak in the closet
pinging in a cake pan.

IV

MORE TROUBLE WITH THE
OBVIOUS

A baby bird has fallen from its tree and lies feebly peeping
dead center of the bright circle under our streetlight.
What is there to do but bring it in? We dutifully prepare a
shoebox, then mix up the baby food and hamburger of an
old routine we know by heart, the ritual we've learned as
children—but the truth is, in all the years since child-
hood, neither my wife nor I can remember having saved
a single bird. We won't save this one either, trembling
weakly now on the kitchen table, refusing to do so much
as open its beak for our ridiculous food.

It lives with us two days, then dies suddenly in my
hand—of "heart attack" my neighbor says. "Young birds
like that almost always die of heart attack." He says this
pounding nails in his porch and I believe him. In fact, I
feel stupid for having mentioned it at all. A heart attack.
Of course. The best thing would have been not to touch
it. Perhaps it would have found a place to hide; and then,
in the morning, its mother might have flown down to
feed it. In any case, it's dead now and buried in the
garden. The same garden, by the way, from which my
neighbor's cat wrestled a live snake once into the hubbub
of our barbecue.

But then I seem to have always had trouble with the
obvious. Once, when a friend died, and after my parents
had told me he had died, I came around the next morning
anyway to call him out for school. His mother came to
the door weeping and told me Orville couldn't go to
school that day. I felt as if I had been walking in my sleep.
I knew my parents hadn't lied, and I certainly knew what

death meant; but somehow, until that moment, I must have thought it was just a dream I'd had. At school, another friend said he thought Orville died from eating donuts every night for supper. I had no trouble at all believing that. By then, donuts made about as much sense as anything.

A baby bird has fallen from its tree . . . someone you love perhaps is dying in another city. There must be something we can do. I remember one Sunday Orville and I got down on our knees in an alley and asked the Blessed Mother for a kite. When we found a rolled-up kite in the next ashcan with the rubber bands still on it, we *knew* it was a miracle. And we were glad, of course; but neither one of us, I think, was overwhelmed. We just believed in miracles and thought they happened all the time. We thought the birds we found needed milk and bread. We thought when they got big they would be our friends, do us wonderful favors, and keep us company forever.

PAINTING THE PICTURE

—for James G. Davis

He had a good job
the kid was no problem
and when he compared the way
his parents had to live
this was nothing, a picnic
and like he told his wife
all he really had to do
was relax, hang loose, learn
to take things easy . . .

but the doctor only nodded
and showed him more pictures.
"How do you feel about this one"
he'd say, and when he said
the doctor wrote it down.
He needed a drink, right now.
It was hard to think right now
about the pictures, the picnic
one especially—why the tree,
for instance, aspired now
in its longest branch
to be the melting snowcap
of a mountain, or exactly
why the flat white woman
asleep there on the blanket
beside her flat-faced husband
had only one arm. The food
looked ridiculous: turkey
cupcakes, ham, too much
of everything—the ice cream

spilling from the baby's bowl
too pink, too visceral. "This
is just a picnic" he said,
"a family having fun." Still,
his wife was in the hospital
wasn't she? Was that the truth?
And then there was the baby
to consider, the terrified
pink baby, the hysterical
toy dog, and everything tilted
toward the immediate foreground
haunted by a hubcap
reflecting something worse.
He wasn't fooling anybody.
He wasn't going home.

WALKING THE BABY TO THE
LIQUOR STORE

It's nearly ten o'clock in the morning and I have work to do. I have to write a novel and a book of criticism. I have also a book of Mongolian double sestinas to translate, a verse play that needs a final act, and a movie script that's hardly off the ground. Besides that, I haven't published a book of my own poetry in weeks, so it's absolutely imperative that I get busy. But first, first I have to take the baby to the liquor store. A brilliant career is one thing —but being a good father, that's what *really* counts.

The baby adores going to the liquor store. In her infant mind there is, perhaps, nothing so beautiful or significant in this world as sitting up in her yellow stroller and rolling bravely west toward some exotically remote BUNNY'S —or, on Sundays, a place as unimaginably far away as KIRBY'S LIQUOR. Such, at least, is the radiant dignity of her expression. And when that snarling German Pinscher throws himself, all teeth and slather, against the pigeon lady's fence on Maple Street, she doesn't turn a hair. Why should she? This morning she's Cleopatra and the liquor store is Rome.

Believe me, I wouldn't miss these excursions for the world. I wouldn't miss them even if it meant giving up the National Book Award. How much trouble is it, after all, to go out walking with the baby? How much work could one possibly do in that brief half-hour? And measured against such joy, such pure infant bliss (which may well indeed anticipate a lifetime's happiness), how important is it that I go to work at all? Sometimes, when we get home from the liquor store, the baby and I are so happy we even do the dishes and have a drink, by God, right there in the kitchen.

The baby knows four words: mommy, daddy, banana and doggy. Could anyone write a novel more interesting than that? It's something I think about often in the glittering fluorescent kitchen after the baby's gone to sleep. And who knows what she'll come up with next? Luckily enough for me, the rigorous disciplines of my craft have trained me in patience. I can probably wait until tomorrow before going to the liquor store again. I can probably fall asleep on the porch tonight like any tired father in mid-career—watching the fireflies coming on and going out again in the long grass like so many sparks flying off the anvil of the world.

CRABAPPLES

Somewhere in the Midwest
crabapples are falling

on a new Buick; crabapples
are littering the sidewalk

and a man is muttering darkly
to himself. It's not pleasant

to contemplate these crabapples.
Ordinarily he'd be having fun

oiling the doors of his Buick
in perfect silence. But not today.

No sir. Not with these crabapples
falling. Not with the driveway

looking like this. He oils up
and slams both Buick doors

then opens up his trunk
and removes a brand-new yellow

plastic garbage can. Perfect.
It's the perfect thing. Now

he must carefully cut up
his old plastic garbage can

and toss it piece by piece
into his new one. It's important

not to hurry and that each piece
be exactly four inches square.

It's important to do things right.
After all, he's got himself

a nice place there. Occasionally
a crabapple hits the roof

trunk or hood of his Buick
or bounces on the driveway

but basically it's a nice place
a good life. Crabapples, insomnia

tumors the size of someone's
little finger? That's nothing.

That's why he stays up past midnight
raking the driveway.

V

DRIVING INTO ENID

—for Louis Jenkins

Hundreds of migrating hawks are roosting in the hedge-rows around Enid, Oklahoma. If the sun were out you could see they were a reddish-brown and had creamy, speckled bellies. But today it's raining in Enid and the rain is mixed with snow. The hawks are merely silhouettes today, far off.

On sunny days, driving into Enid might easily remind you of a scene in a grade-school geography book: behind the hawk on the fencepost, a train goes speeding toward some grain elevators on the outskirts of the city . . . then the horizon, and an airplane flying low over a few tall buildings. But today the winter grasses tremble on the hillsides and the scarce trees tremble.

I was just thinking I had come a long way . . . I was just thinking that next year, for sure, I'd buy a new car. I must have been thinking something like that on the outskirts, passing the first small factories, the ragged fields strewn with junk. . . .

Then, at the first stoplight, some kid waves at me from the back seat of a police car . . . inscrutable, fierce. He looks like a kid I knew in grade school. His mother wore a fur coat in the middle of summer and believed the Russians were shooting tornadoes at us.

What did he do? Where are they taking him? They found him in a culvert trying to gut a chicken with a piece of glass . . . they found him trying to build a fire out of cow-shit and wet sticks. They found him all right and now he's going back.

Later on, I'll find his sister quite by accident selling cameras in the discount store. She has a crooked, shy face and reddish-brown hair. She's married now and her chewed fingers are tatooed SUE on one hand DAVE on the other.

RANCHO LINDA VISTA

Fated. Doomed. Inexorable.
You know the story.

Things go along just fine
until the chickens die.

Then the sheep die
half the barn caves in

and one dusty afternoon
the children step down

from the school bus
and disappear. Senile

dementia. The tarantula plant.
The cactus with yellow eyes.

That peculiar ambience
in which a future bangs around

like an old windmill
and says *goodbye, goodbye*

all day. An atmosphere
redolent of old ladies

who can't speak English
talking to the ants

shouting at the airplanes.
Cancer. Dogshit. The bullsnake

climbing up the drainpipe.
Whatever life does to us

whatever life does to us
until one feels sorry even

for the beautiful coyotes
who step in broad daylight

across the fallen-down corrals
looking for the sheep.

DO NOT DUMP DEAD ANIMALS

—Oracle, Arizona, 1976

Here at the Oracle dump the dumping of dead animals is strictly forbidden—and for my part I think it's a good idea. I can see this means to be a nice dump and that it wouldn't take many dead animals to subvert that intention. Live animals, however, are excused. Cows, for instance, by accident or design, are to be found nosing through the garbage all over the place—huge cows with red eyes and filthy muzzles. But honk your horn, shout at them, and they'll fix you with a look so full of bliss, so void of all suspicion, mere humans are forced to look away. If this were heaven, in other words, these cows might pass for angels. No cow in India, I think, could look more perfectly at home.

I rather like it here myself. I like the cratered, smoking, heaped-up aspect of the place, the kitchen sink irony of it all. What's a perfectly good artificial leg, for instance, doing in the shotgunned stove? And who owned the violin full of Eisenhower buttons? I like the festive way old wire, underwear, innertubes, newspaper, bread wrappers, toilet paper, paper bags, rags, ribbons of bright plastic animate the shattered trees—and of course I like the cows too. If this really were a kind of heaven, would it be so bad to come back here as a cow? When I ask a cow that question she just stares at me, puzzled, drooling little strings of green slime. What does she care? She stares at me so long I almost offer her an apology. Do you suppose the dead are like this? Perhaps they really do hear us, but from their vantage in paradise any answer they might make seems to them all nonsense and forgone.

The Oracle dump is on high ground and when the wind is right you can look out over the desert for miles in any direction. Today, I can read the letters on the Magma Copper smokestack down in San Manuel. I can make out the toy cars shining in the parking lot—and when the shift whistle blows, I can follow a few small trails of dust almost to the mountains surrounding Tucson. Other cars grow larger as they speed across the valley toward trailer courts in Oracle or Mammoth. And sometimes a car turns off the Oracle road and heads up here toward the dump. This time it's a young woman in a dusty pickup. She parks beside me and gets out with a rifle. Then she tries to coax a cat out from under the front seat. "Come here," she says, "come here sweetheart."

I can see she wants me to help her. I can see she would rather not have to do this thing but feels, perhaps, that the dumping of sick, live animals is cowardly and cruel. Now she is down on her hands and knees angling for a clear shot underneath the truck . . . I can hear her crying. She sounds like someone who has tried and tried but can't light the pilot underneath the stove. The washing machine is broken and she can't fix it. How will she pay the rent? Huge cows track up the kitchen, wreck the living room. But rules are rules, after all, so I go on pretending to be a worried man looking for something important: a bill of sale thrown out inadvertently, a priceless heirloom, the letter that might finally prove my innocence.

VI

ARIZONA MOVIES

1

Rosetta, her new boy friend
and all four kids
are going to the drive-in
down in San Manuel.

"One more beer," they tell the kids
"and then we'll go." The kids
want a quarter a nickel
another dime—the kids

are a pain in the ass
the movie is about a dog
and the boy friend wears glasses
baggy double-knit slacks

and a white belt. Rosetta,
on the other hand, is beautiful,
elegant, altogether sweet
in her new blue sweater

and when she reaches in her purse
to buy another round,
I spot her little silver gun.
"That's just in case," she says,

"just in case."

2

Sometimes
even in the middle
of the year's best movie

you can hear coyotes
at the San Manuel Drive-in.

Tonight, they are far away
and merely barking at the moon . . .

but Rosetta tells me
that when they chorus close
and suddenly together

hysterical, high-pitched, furious

it means something is dying
in the dark foothills
behind the shaky screen.

3
After the bad movie
Rosetta wants to finish off
what's left of the tequila
drop off the kids

and then go dancing. . . !

But I don't know about Fred.
I think Fred sells mobile homes —
convenient, air-conditioned,
catastrophically fragile,

I pass them every day
and try to imagine myself
living there: the TV on
all the kids at school

and Rosetta just lying
on the couch, just watching,
through the picture window,
some Apache ghost dance

cavalry of thunderheads
advancing slowly out
from between Mount Lemmon

and a pigeon-blue wing
of the Catalinas.

4
No one is dancing
up at Pop-A-Tops. No one
is speaking. The TV's on
and in the Merry Christmas

snow-flaked mirror, Fred
is shooting pool. Rosetta,
on the other hand, shreds
her matches into tiny bits

then looking up, her look
slides sidelong into mine —

the tense, unsteady look
I think, of children

getting lost . . . but what
was it that I thought to say?
Something dumb, mindless
a remark about the movie

or at my best, to notice
on that long small arm
her careful, barroom bracelet
of pink and yellow straws.

Whatever it was, she answers
to the whole place —loud,
and before I say a word:
"Nope, I'm not dead yet"

and the fuzzed-up mirror
keeps still, stays quiet
as the slow blue echo
of a pistol shot.

5
Rosetta says she's 32
but Fred looks younger.
Fred's even younger partner
works the graveyard shift

at Magma Copper
and behind us all

the Falstaff clock
turns counterclockwise

towards eleven. "One more game,"
they tell Rosetta, "and then
we'll go." *The Lariat?*
The Hangman's Tree?

"Why not Rosetta's place?"
Fred's partner whispers.
A joke perhaps. But still
it's curious, frightening

that I should also hear
in the shy nylon whisper
of Rosetta's thighs
in the click of small ice

something dangerous, random,
confused as kitchens,
cupboards where the knives
are kept, bedrooms

in the Apache Trailer Court
with real bullet holes
above the door.

6
Like Rosetta
I too hear voices.

Tonight, they are speaking
the frazzled language

of neon, the cindered
impossible language

of parking lots, static
and revolving lights . . .

but sometimes, it's Rosetta —
her voice still angry

clear, above the voices
of the graveyard shift

who slam their doors
like Fred or anyone

going off half drunk
to work tonight

in knee-deep water
and the hot acidic dark

one full mile
underground.

POETRY FROM ILLINOIS

History Is Your Own
Heartbeat
Michael S. Harper (1971)

The Foreclosure
Richard Emil Braun (1972)

The Scrawny Sonnets and
Other Narratives
Robert Bagg (1973)

The Creation Frame
Phyllis Thompson (1973)

To All Appearances: Poems
New and Selected
Josephine Miles (1974)

Nightmare Begins
Responsibility
Michael S. Harper (1975)

The Black Hawk Songs
Michael Borich (1975)

The Wichita Poems
Michael Van Walleghen
(1975)

Cumberland Station
Dave Smith (1977)

Tracking
Virginia R. Terris (1977)

Poems of the Two Worlds
Frederick Morgan (1977)

Images of Kin: New and
Selected Poems
Michael S. Harper (1977)

On Earth As It Is
Dan Masterson (1978)

Riversongs
Michael Anania (1978)

Goshawk, Antelope
Dave Smith (1979)

Death Mother and Other
Poems
Frederick Morgan (1979)

Local Men
James Whitehead (1979)

Coming to Terms
Josephine Miles (1979)

Searching the Drowned Man
Sydney Lea (1980)

With Akhmatova at the
Black Gates
Stephen Berg (1981)

More Trouble with the
Obvious
Michael Van Walleghen (1981)

A Note on the Author

MICHAEL VAN WALLEGHEN, associate professor of English at the University of Illinois at Urbana-Champaign, is the author of *The Wichita Poems*. A native of Detroit, Van Walleghen is a graduate of Wayne State University and the Writer's Workshop at the University of Iowa. He has won the Pushcart Prize, a Borestone Mountain Poetry Award, an Illinois Arts Council Award, and a Literature Fellowship from the National Endowment for the Arts.